W9-AWX-566

JOHN DONOVAN LIBRARY
Madison Central School
Madison, New York 13402

Art Director	Charles Matheson
Art Editor	Ben White
Editor	James McCarter
Illustrators	Chris Forsey
	Hayward Art Group
	Jim Robins

© Aladdin Books Ltd

Designed and produced by
Aladdin Books Ltd
70 Old Compton St
London W1

*First published in the
United States 1984 by*
Franklin Watts
387 Park Avenue South
New York 10016

ISBN 0-531-04837-3
Library of Congress
Catalog Card No: 84-50608

Printed in Belgium
All rights reserved

612

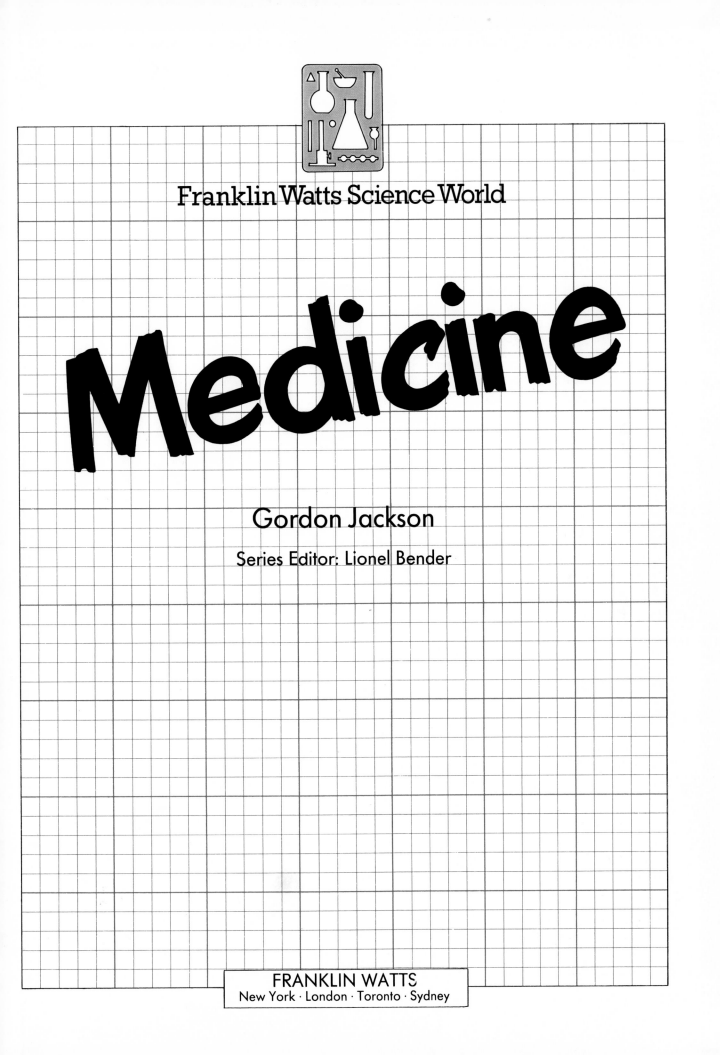

Franklin Watts Science World

Medicine

Gordon Jackson

Series Editor: Lionel Bender

FRANKLIN WATTS
New York · London · Toronto · Sydney

Introduction

The study of the structure and function of the human body is one of the most fascinating areas of science. After all, the body is something that concerns all of us. This book explores the structure and function of the major systems of the body, beginning with a look at the way muscles, bones and joints work together to allow us to move about, and then at the workings of the heart, lungs and blood.

Most people have only a hazy idea about the organs that they carry about inside them. This book describes their function in digestion and nutrition, and the way food eventually ends up at the body's cells to be used as fuel. Finally, it looks at the brain and the nervous system as well as the sense organs, which are perhaps the areas we all find most interesting, since they are so bound up with the way we think and feel.

The last part of the book is concerned with some of the main causes of illness and how the body deals with infection. It explains the way in which medical scientists use their knowledge to try to prevent disease. In recent years, doctors and scientists have become very interested in the way the body is designed to deal with the threat of infection. This has led to a better understanding of how the body's defenses deal with and even prevent disease. The book ends with a look at the ways in which some diseases have been effectively controlled and even eradicated.

Medicine is a subject that deals with the body, both in illness and in health. To understand our bodies, we need to look carefully at the structure of the various organs and systems. At the same time, it is essential to see how they function, especially when extra demands are made on them, as there are when we play sports, for example. Doctors use this knowledge in both the diagnosis and in the treatment of disease, using techniques like surgery. However, it is always better to try to prevent illness rather than to try to cure it when its symptoms are felt.

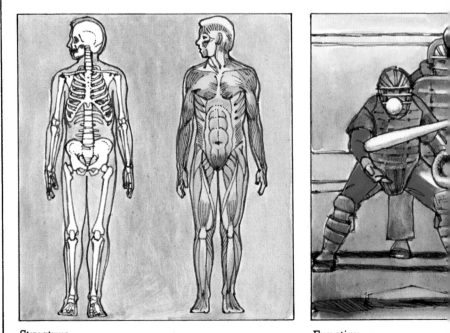

Structure   Function

Contents

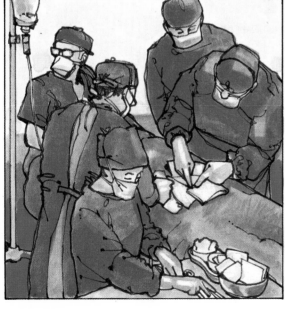

Treatment

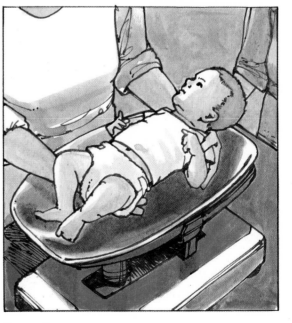

Prevention

Support and Movement

The skills that soccer players show on the field are the result of long hours of practice and training. Their skills depend on the precise control of the movements of different parts of their bodies. Every movement they make is the result of the action of a number of different muscles, whether it is a quick glance to find a teammate or a powerful kick at the goal.

All the movements we make result from the action of muscles on our basic framework – the skeleton. The skeleton is made up of more than 200 individual bones that are joined together by different types of joints. The joints must be strong enough to withstand the strains that we put on them, and flexible enough to allow us to move freely.

Our muscles, and the bones they move, are in constant action, even when we think that we are doing nothing at all. Anyone who has watched the tremendous effort a toddler makes when he or she is learning to stand up, will realize that a lot of muscle effort is needed just to overcome the effects of gravity, and to maintain balance.

Some muscles, such as those in our backs, arms and legs, are large and powerful, giving us the strength to run, jump, and lift heavy weights. Others, like those in our hands and fingers, allow precise, controlled movements. In all, our bones and muscles make up well over half of our total body weight.

▷ Athletes need to be in peak physical condition. Everything that these soccer players are doing depends upon the precise control of their movements, and during the course of a game they will use most of the muscles in their bodies. When the ball is "headed," for example, the muscles of the legs, back, abdomen, neck and head all come into play.

Skeleton and muscle

If we were not supported by our bones we would collapse on the ground in a shapeless, rubbery heap! The skeleton is the framework around which our bodies are built. It also gives protection: the bony skull protects the brain, while the rib cage protects the heart and lungs. The skeleton is also the platform from which muscles exert their force. Muscles are anchored to bones at each end, and work by pulling away from these anchor points.

The skeletal system

The muscular system

The Skeleton and Muscles

Human beings are symmetrical – we have the same bones and muscles on each side of our bodies. This diagram shows our basic structure. The skull is made of a number of bones fused together. It is supported by a column of 24 vertebrae that make up the spine. At the base of the spine, another five vertebrae join together to form the sacrum to which the bones of the pelvis are attached. The pelvic bones anchor the large thigh and buttock muscles which hold us upright. Both the arms and legs have a single long bone in the upper part and two in the lower part. Seven cube-like bones at the wrist and six at the ankle are connected to the longer bones of the fingers and toes. Each bone is connected to its neighbor by bands of tough, flexible fiber called ligaments. Other long fibers, called tendons, anchor muscles to the bones.

Muscles and bones

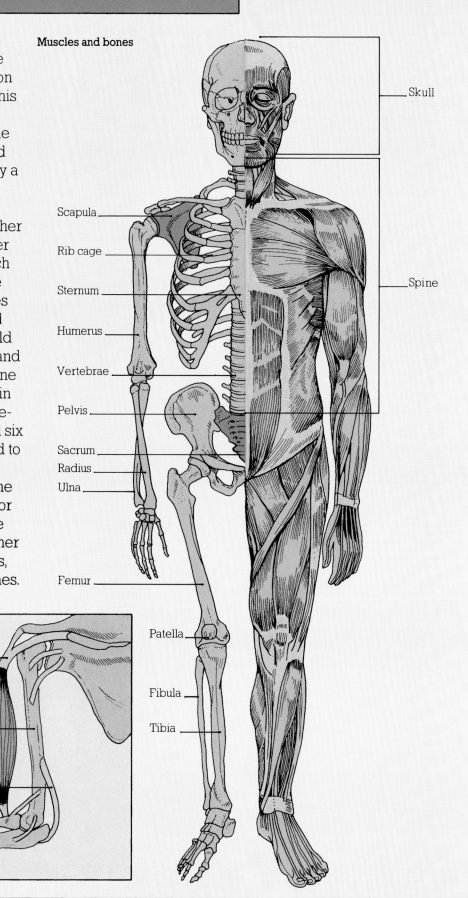

Skull

Scapula

Rib cage

Sternum

Humerus

Vertebrae

Pelvis

Sacrum

Radius

Ulna

Spine

Femur

Patella

Fibula

Tibia

Ligaments and tendons

Tendon – muscle to bone

Muscle

Bone

Ligament – bone to bone

Joints

Most joints allow movement in a particular direction only. The knee joint, for example – a hinge joint – allows a bending movement in just one direction. But the ball and socket joint in the hip gives movement in all directions, to a limited extent. The ligaments prevent the joint from moving too far. However, all moving joints have the same basic structure. Where two bones meet, they are covered by a rubbery sheet of fibrous material called cartilage. The cartilage layers glide smoothly over one another.

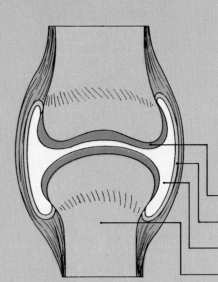

The knee joint

Cartilage

Synovial membrane

Synovial fluid

Bone

A typical joint

To make the joint move more easily, it is lubricated by the synovial fluid that fills the space inside it. The fluid is

made by a special membrane (the synovial membrane) which also forms a watertight seal around the joint.

Movement and Muscles

Muscles are the red, "meaty" parts of our bodies. They are mainly composed of thousands of thin, flexible fibers. Each of these fibers can contract, becoming shorter and thicker, pulling the muscle away from its anchor point to cause movement. You can see this when you bend your arm. The biceps muscle, attached to the scapula at the top and to the lower arm at the bottom, contracts and shortens the distance between the shoulder and lower arm, forcing the arm to bend. To straighten the arm, the biceps muscle relaxes and

the triceps muscle at the back of your arm contracts, pulling the lower arm downward. All of our muscles work in pairs in this way.

Lifting a weight

The major muscles of the arm

Upper arm

Biceps contracts and the arm bends.

Scapula

As the biceps contracts, the triceps relaxes.

Lower arm

The Human Engine

When lumberjacks are felling trees, they use up enormous amounts of energy. In many ways, their bodies are working like the gasoline engines that drive their chain saws. Inside the engine, gasoline is burned with air to produce the energy to saw the wood. Much the same thing happens in the body, although food rather than gasoline is burned inside the body's cells. And like the gasoline engine, the body cells need air, or more specifically, oxygen, to burn the food and produce the energy that is needed to keep the body working.

The purpose of breathing is to move air in and out of the lungs. Once air is inside the lungs, the oxygen in the air is taken into the bloodstream. Although the blood has many functions, one of its most important jobs is to carry oxygen from the lungs to each of the body's cells. When the oxygen has been used up, the waste product – carbon dioxide – is carried in the blood back through the heart to the lungs, and breathed out into the air. When we are sitting still, we normally breathe in and out about 16 times a minute, but this rate increases dramatically when we are working or taking exercise.

The heart pumps oxygen-rich blood through its system of blood vessels from the lungs to the cells where the oxygen is needed. The used blood is returned to the lungs to pick up more oxygen from them for further circulation.

▷ As these men work, their cells burn fuel to provide them with energy for their activities. In the process, enough extra heat is produced to make the men hot, even on a cold day.

Blood and breathing

Air is drawn into the lungs through the windpipe, or trachea. The oxygen-rich blood from the lungs goes to the heart, where it is pumped through blood vessels called arteries (red) to the rest of the body. The arteries branch to eventually form a network of tiny vessels called capillaries. These feed all the body's cells. Used blood is returned to the heart through the veins (blue) and then pumped back to the lungs for more oxygen.

Respiratory system

Circulatory system

11

Breathing

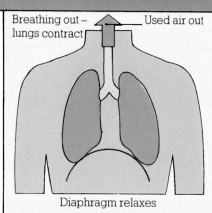

Breathing out – lungs contract — Used air out

Diaphragm relaxes

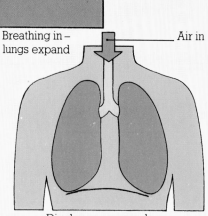

Breathing in – lungs expand — Air in

Diaphragm moves down

Breathing hard

If you place your hands on the sides of your chest and take a deep breath in, you can feel your chest move upward and outward. When you breathe out, it goes down and in. The rib cage expands as you breathe in; the lungs expand to fill the space and draw in air through the nose and mouth.

The diaphragm is a sheet of muscle that lies beneath the lungs. It is dome-shaped, but flattens when you breathe in, making more space into which the lungs expand. You can often see your stomach getting bigger as you breathe in, as the diaphragm pushes down upon it.

Normally, all the effort of breathing happens during the breathing-in stage. Breathing out occurs as the muscles of the rib cage and diaphragm relax and return to their normal places. Only when you are really short of breath do you *force* air out so you can take the next breath more quickly.

Oxygen and Blood

The lungs are like two spongy balloons. The air is drawn into them through the windpipe, which branches to supply each lung. It then passes into smaller air passages which end in tiny clusters of air sacs, called alveoli. They are rather like minute bunches of air-filled grapes. Wrapped around the outside of the alveoli are the tiny capillaries which carry blood. Their walls are very thin, so that oxygen can pass easily into the blood, and waste carbon dioxide carried by used blood can pass easily out.

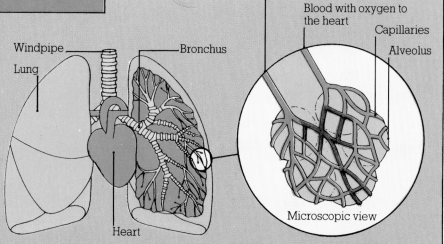

Windpipe

Lung

Bronchus

Blood without oxygen to the alveoli

Blood with oxygen to the heart

Capillaries

Alveolus

Heart

Microscopic view

The millions of tiny alveoli in the lungs make up a huge surface through which oxygen and carbon dioxide can pass. In fact, the lung's surface laid out flat would be about as big as a tennis court.

Our lungs are never completely emptied of air. In quiet breathing, only about ten percent of the air in the lungs is breathed out, but this is enough to supply the oxygen we need.

The Circulatory System

Each cell needs its supply of oxygen-rich blood, and it is the job of the heart and the arteries to supply it. The veins, which carry the blood on its return journey to the heart, usually run alongside the arteries. The circulation of blood has other functions apart from just supplying oxygen. Blood carries digested food to the tissues and it also carries chemical waste products away from the tissues to the kidneys, from where they are removed from the body.

Blood pressure

The strongest pumping chamber of the heart has to force blood out at quite a high pressure, to force it through the arterial system to the capillaries. You can count your heartbeats – your "pulse" – and feel the force of this pumping when you press your fingers on the artery at your wrist.

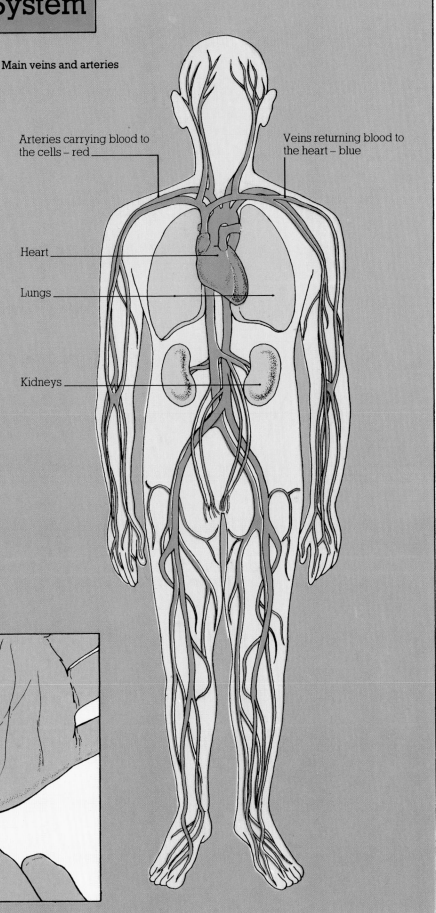

Main veins and arteries

Arteries carrying blood to the cells – red

Veins returning blood to the heart – blue

Heart

Lungs

Kidneys

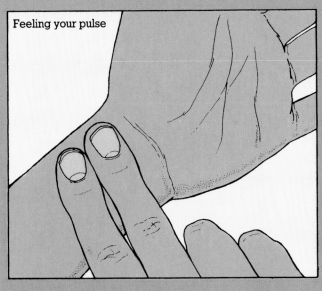

Feeling your pulse

The Blood

Blood consists of millions of tiny cells floating in a straw-colored fluid called plasma. The red color comes from the red blood cells, which actually carry the oxygen and carbon dioxide in the blood. The white blood cells are bigger than the red cells, but there are far fewer of them. They protect the body against infection by attacking any germs that get into the blood-stream. The platelets are the smallest cells. They plug up any holes if a blood vessel is damaged and help to make the blood clot, preventing too much blood loss.

The body makes blood inside the center of certain bones, and so can replace small losses. But major losses require an urgent transfusion of blood from healthy donors.

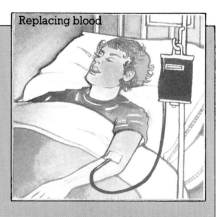
Replacing blood

Red blood cells
These are the cells that carry oxygen from the lungs to the rest of the body. They then carry some carbon dioxide back to the lungs.

Platelets
Platelets have a sticky surface. They gather at a wound to stop bleeding and work with other substances in the plasma to form blood clots.

White blood cells
These are the mainstay of the body's protection against infection. There are two main types, called lymphocytes and phagocytes.

Plasma
This is the fluid in which the cells float. Many of the body's important chemicals are dissolved in and carried in the plasma.

The Heart

The heart's muscular walls give it the power to pump blood around the body. The heart has two separate halves. Each half has an upper chamber, or atrium, which receives incoming blood. This blood passes into the main pumping chambers – the ventricles – during the resting period between each heartbeat. The right-hand side of the heart receives blood from the tissues and pumps it to the lungs. The blood returns to the left-hand side of the heart, where the left ventricle, the heart's most powerful chamber, pumps it out to the arteries to supply the rest of the body.

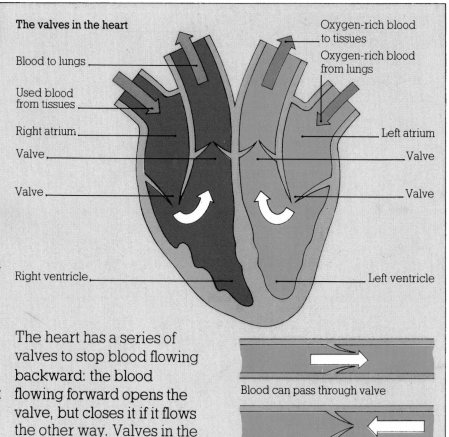

The valves in the heart

Blood to lungs

Used blood from tissues

Right atrium

Valve

Valve

Right ventricle

Oxygen-rich blood to tissues

Oxygen-rich blood from lungs

Left atrium

Valve

Valve

Left ventricle

The heart has a series of valves to stop blood flowing backward: the blood flowing forward opens the valve, but closes it if it flows the other way. Valves in the veins work in a similar way.

Blood can pass through valve

Valve closes if blood flows back

Heart Problems

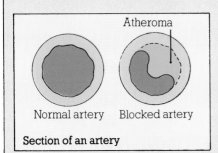

Atheroma

Normal artery   Blocked artery

Section of an artery

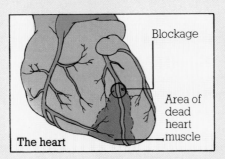

Blockage

Area of dead heart muscle

The heart

Unblocking the pipes!

An adult's heart beats about 70 times per minute (in children the rate is slightly higher). The heart is one of our most important organs, so heart disease can be especially serious. The most common of heart diseases is caused by a thickening of the arteries that supply it with blood. Over a long period, a fatty porridge-like substance called atheroma may build up on the inside wall of the artery. This is rather like deposits forming on the inside of a waterpipe, blocking the pipe.

In a similar way, when the walls of the artery thicken, blood cannot flow normally. If the fatty deposits in a coronary (heart) artery become very thick, blood stops flowing into part of the heart muscle. As that part becomes starved of blood, it dies, and the heart stops working. This is what happens in a heart attack.

Lung Problems

The body can only get all the oxygen it needs to function well when the lungs are healthy. In a condition called emphysema, the delicate walls of the alveoli are broken down. When this happens, the air sacs enlarge, but the lungs lose some of their total surface area. This means that they cannot supply the blood with enough oxygen, and the patient becomes breathless, even when walking. In another lung disease, called chronic bronchitis, the lining of the air passages becomes thickened. This reduces the amount of air that can reach the alveoli.

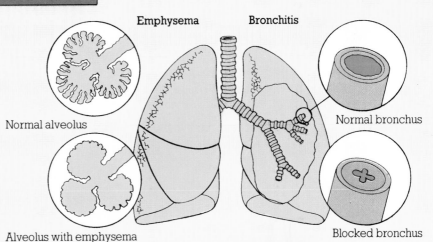

Emphysema   Bronchitis

Normal alveolus

Normal bronchus

Alveolus with emphysema

Blocked bronchus

The most common cause of both these lung diseases is cigarette smoking. Cigarette smoking has also been shown to be one of the major causes of heart disease. In fact, it is one of the most important causes of ill-health in Western countries today.

Cigarettes are dangerous!

Diet and Digestion

We all need food to keep us going and give us the energy we need for everyday activities. Although people in the various parts of the world eat an enormous variety of foods, all food is made up of only three main substances: carbohydrate, protein and fat, together with small amounts of vitamins and minerals and, of course, water.

Carbohydrates are the starchy and sugary foods that are our main source of energy. Proteins are essential for the healthy growth and repair of damaged tissues. Fats (including oils) also provide energy and, in small quantities, are needed for growth and body repair. In addition, we also need very small amounts of vitamins and minerals. These keep the thousands of chemical processes that take place in every cell of the body working properly. Our diet should contain a balance of all these different substances, to keep us healthy.

When we eat food, we grind it with our teeth and then swallow it, so that it passes down into the stomach. Here, it begins to be digested – broken down into the basic chemicals of which it is made. This process continues in the small intestine, from where the basic constituents of the food are absorbed into the body. Other chemical changes may occur in the liver, before the food is passed on in the bloodstream to the cells, where it acts as fuel or as the building material for new tissues.

◁ A healthy meal contains the correct balance of carbohydrates, proteins and fats. Fresh food also provides the necessary vitamins and minerals, as well as the fiber that helps the intestines to work properly.

Carbohydrates

Sugar is the basic ingredient of carbohydrate foods. When many sugar particles join together, they form starch, the basis of foods such as flour, bread and rice. A healthy diet should be based on starchy foods rather than those containing pure sugar.

Fats and oils

Meat, cooking and salad oils, butter, margarine, whole milk and cream, are all sources of fat. Some fat is essential in the diet, but too much can be harmful. Fat from animals, rather than that from vegetables, seems to increase the risk of heart disease.

Protein

Meat, poultry, fish and eggs are the main sources of protein in most Western diets. But some vegetables, such as beans, are even richer in protein. Our cells are mainly built of protein, so protein is essential for repair and growth, although it can also be burned as fuel.

Vitamins and minerals

There are many different essential vitamins and minerals, and they are all provided in a well-balanced diet. Fresh, uncooked vegetables, fruit, and fish are good sources of most vitamins. Vitamin D is created in the body by the action of sunlight on the skin.

The Digestive System

Before our bodies can use the food we eat, it must be digested. First it is chewed and mixed with saliva. This is a clear fluid from the salivary glands which begins to break the food down. Once the food is swallowed it passes into the stomach, where it is churned around and mixed with the stomach's acid and juices. It then moves to the duodenum – the first part of the small intestine – where other digestive juices from the pancreas and gall bladder are added to the mixture. These break the food down further so that it can be absorbed into the bloodstream as it passes along the small intestine. The wastes pass through the large intestine and are excreted.

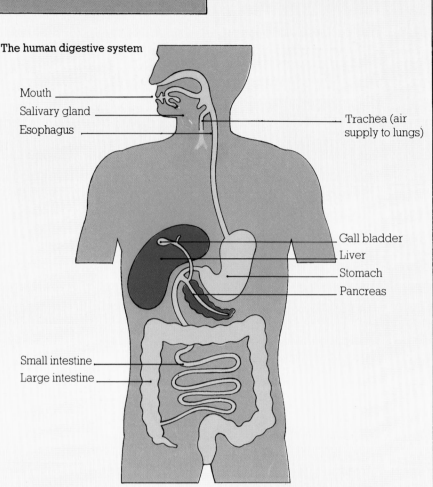

The human digestive system

- Mouth
- Salivary gland
- Esophagus
- Trachea (air supply to lungs)
- Gall bladder
- Liver
- Stomach
- Pancreas
- Small intestine
- Large intestine

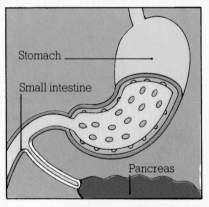

Stomach
Small intestine
Pancreas

The stomach
Saliva begins to break down starches, but the real chemical attack on food starts as food is mixed in the stomach with the stomach acid. Chemicals called enzymes work on the proteins, breaking them down into smaller particles.

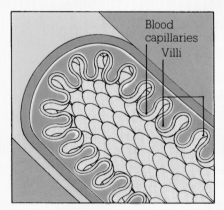

Blood capillaries
Villi

The small intestine
After the food has been chemically split up by acid and enzymes, it can be absorbed by the blood vessels in the small intestine. The intestine has millions of tiny finger-like projections called villi, which increase the area where food is absorbed.

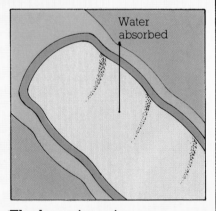

Water absorbed

The large intestine
As food moves down the small intestine, it is completely fluid. Some fluid is taken up into the blood in the small intestine, but most is removed in the large intestine. The remaining semi-solid material is passed out of the body.

Food for Cells

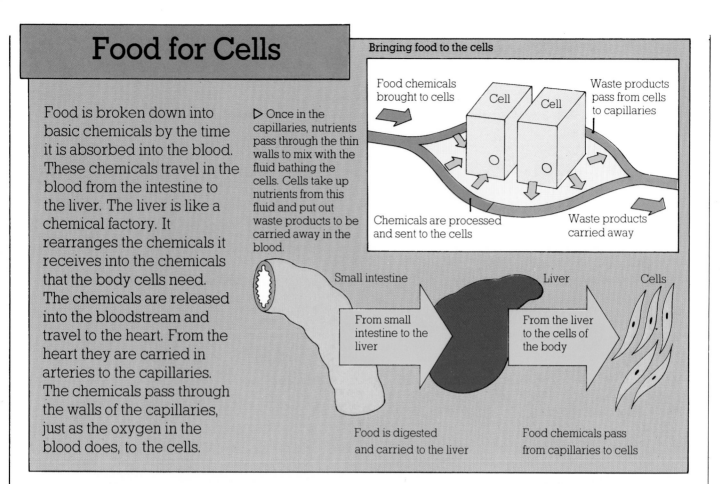

Bringing food to the cells

Food chemicals brought to cells

Cell

Cell

Waste products pass from cells to capillaries

Chemicals are processed and sent to the cells

Waste products carried away

Small intestine

Liver

Cells

From small intestine to the liver

From the liver to the cells of the body

Food is digested and carried to the liver

Food chemicals pass from capillaries to cells

Food is broken down into basic chemicals by the time it is absorbed into the blood. These chemicals travel in the blood from the intestine to the liver. The liver is like a chemical factory. It rearranges the chemicals it receives into the chemicals that the body cells need. The chemicals are released into the bloodstream and travel to the heart. From the heart they are carried in arteries to the capillaries. The chemicals pass through the walls of the capillaries, just as the oxygen in the blood does, to the cells.

▷ Once in the capillaries, nutrients pass through the thin walls to mix with the fluid bathing the cells. Cells take up nutrients from this fluid and put out waste products to be carried away in the blood.

Burning Food For Energy

Relaxing

Light exercise

Using more energy

We need energy to keep us warm, to move our muscles and to fuel the many chemical processes that take place in our bodies. Inside cells, nutrients such as fats and carbohydrates react with the oxygen supplied by breathing. The reaction releases energy and also produces carbon dioxide, which passes back into the blood, to be returned to the lungs. The energy available from foods is measured in units called calories. An adult man uses about two calories per minute just to keep his body systems working properly. But the more work or exercise we do, the more energy we need. Walking slowly uses about three calories a minute. Running up stairs requires about 20 calories. Any food that we eat in excess of our energy requirements is stored as fat, which can be converted to energy when needed.

Removing Wastes

All the chemical activities that go on in the body's cells produce chemical waste products that must be disposed of if the body is to remain healthy. The kidneys and urinary system are one of the main pathways for excretion of waste. As the blood is pumped out of the heart into the body, a large proportion of it is directed through the kidneys. Here it is filtered, and the urine that is produced by this process contains most of the waste products and some of the water from the plasma. The urine then passes down the two ureters to collect in the bladder. This is a muscular bag that passes urine out of the body through the urethra.

Maintaining a balance

Although the kidneys have a very important role in getting rid of waste, they also have a vital job to do in keeping in balance the levels of important substances in the blood, such as salt and water. The cells of the body depend upon having a constant level of both salt and water to allow their delicate chemical activities to work normally. This balance depends on many circumstances. For example, if you drink a lot of water on a cold day, the body will pass a lot of it out in urine. But on a hot day this water will be lost as sweat, so the kidneys will adjust by making less urine.

Organs of excretion

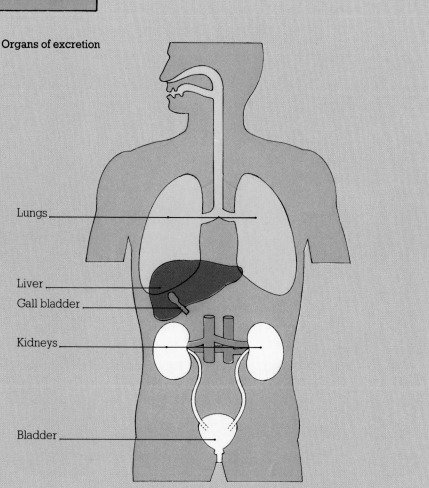

Lungs

Liver

Gall bladder

Kidneys

Bladder

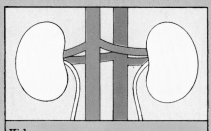

Kidneys
The kidneys balance the amount of salt and water in the body, and excrete waste products.

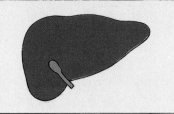

Liver
The liver maintains the balance of many important chemicals, including sugar and protein.

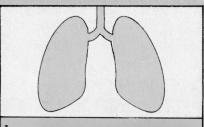

Lungs
The lungs remove carbon dioxide. If carbon dioxide accumulates, the body becomes too acid.

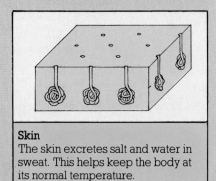

Skin
The skin excretes salt and water in sweat. This helps keep the body at its normal temperature.

20

The Chemical Messengers

There are many chemical activities going on in the cells of the body and they all have to be controlled so that the body functions as a whole. This control is maintained by the hormones. Hormones are chemical messengers that are carried in the bloodstream. They are produced by the endocrine glands and act on each individual cell.

Hormones are especially important in controlling the process of reproduction and in producing the different characteristics of men and women. The whole system is governed by the pituitary gland, which influences the activity of the other glands. It also produces hormones that control growth and the body's water balance.

The other glands

Endocrine glands release their hormones directly into the bloodstream. The thyroid gland lies in the neck. It controls the overall level of energy used by the body's cells. Lying just behind it are four tiny parathyroid glands; their job is to control calcium levels in the bones and in the rest of the body.

The pancreas contains small areas of endocrine tissue that make insulin, the hormone that controls the body's sugar level. The testes in men and the ovaries in women make the sex hormones that control

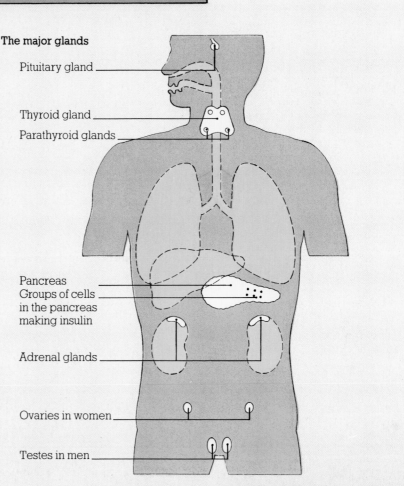

The major glands

Pituitary gland

Thyroid gland

Parathyroid glands

Pancreas

Groups of cells in the pancreas making insulin

Adrenal glands

Ovaries in women

Testes in men

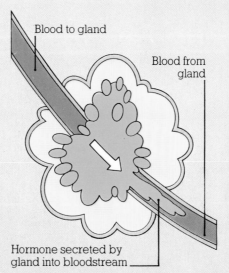

Blood to gland

Blood from gland

Hormone secreted by gland into bloodstream

Emergency stations!

reproduction. The two adrenal glands make the hormones adrenalin and cortisone, both of which help the body respond to stress. Adrenalin prepares the body

for the "fight or flight" reaction, when it is suddenly produced to give us the energy to deal with an emergency. Cortisone acts more slowly to help us cope with stress.

Coordination and Control

These tennis players are very fit, and their muscles are strong. But what sets them apart from most of us is their superb control and coordination of their movements. As they smash the tennis ball back over the net, their skill lies in the coordination of their arms and their eyes.

Every movement we make, whether it is hitting a tennis ball or doing something simple such as getting out of a chair, is controlled by the activity of our nervous systems – the brain, spinal cord and nerves, acting together. The nervous system controls many of the body's automatic functions – the things we do without thinking, such as keeping our hearts beating, or breathing. Breathing, swallowing and the control of the body's temperature are essential to life, and require the continuous activity of the nervous system for their control.

The spinal cord runs down the center of the spine and is protected by the vertebral bones. The nerves emerge from the spinal cord and travel to all parts of the body. Messages travel down single nerve fibers to the part of the body which is to carry out the action required.

Nerves also carry information from the body back to the brain. The brain needs a great deal of information to make even the simplest action. For example, even when we move out of a chair, the brain must know exactly how our muscles are working in order to maintain balance and ensure a smooth movement.

▷ These players can spot the ball, move into position and decide where to hit it within a fraction of a second. Each of these steps requires the coordinated activity of many different parts of the nervous system.

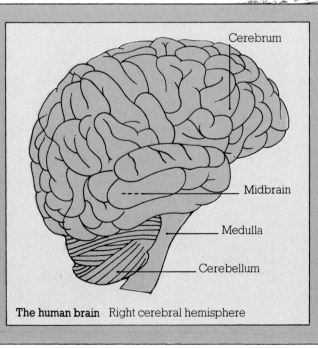

The human brain
This picture shows the brain, seen from the right. Two cerebral hemispheres control voluntary activity. (We can only see one hemisphere since we are looking from the side.) The left hemisphere controls the right hand side of the body and the right hemisphere, the left side. Underneath this are the cerebellum and the midbrain which control involuntary functions and conduct messages out to the body.

Cerebrum

Midbrain

Medulla

Cerebellum

The human brain Right cerebral hemisphere

Of course, the brain has many other functions apart from controlling our movements and body systems. We can think, learn skills, imagine, dream and remember things. Even the most advanced computer has only a fraction of the memory capacity of the human brain, and no computer can think in the creative way that humans can. These "higher" functions of the brain take place in the front part of the brain, but we have only a vague idea of how they work. More than any other organ in our bodies, the brain remains a mystery.

The Nervous System

Messages to and from the brain are actually tiny electrical impulses that are sent along the main nerves of the body. These are divided into two groups: the 12 pairs of cranial nerves that lead from the brain through the skull, and the 31 pairs of spinal nerves that lead from the spinal cord to all other parts of the body. The spinal cord and the brain form the central nervous system; the smaller nerves that split off from the main ones make up the peripheral nervous system.

Nerves are made up of hundreds of microscopic nerve fibers, rather like an electric cable is composed of small wires. The individual fibers are an extension of a single nerve cell. Sometimes the fibers are very long. For example, a fiber in the foot is part of a nerve cell that has its center somewhere near the level of the stomach.

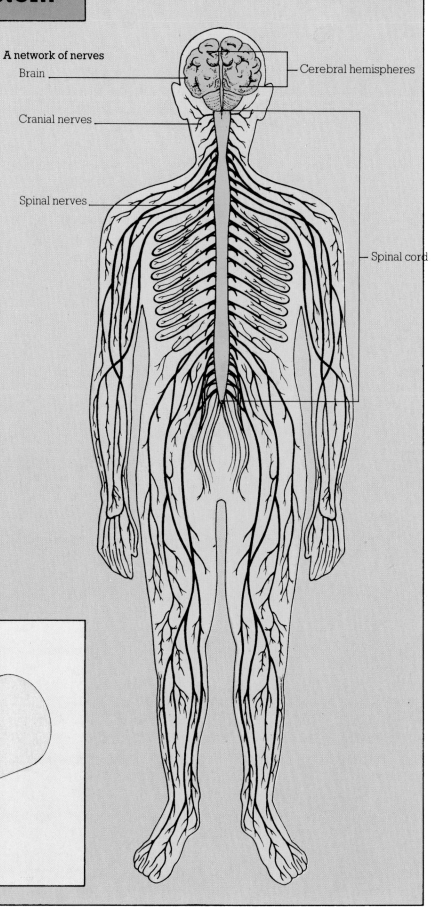

A network of nerves

Brain

Cranial nerves

Spinal nerves

Cerebral hemispheres

Spinal cord

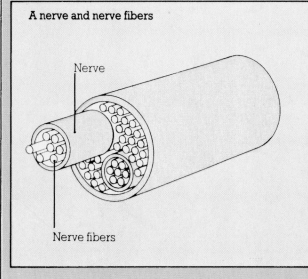

A nerve and nerve fibers

Nerve

Nerve fibers

Automatic Control

Most of the activity of the nervous system is automatic. If you stand on tiptoe on one leg, you will make continuous small movements, even though you are trying to keep still. These are automatic movements, or reflexes, which are necessary to keep you balanced. One simple reflex is the knee jerk. Tapping the leg just below the knee cap suddenly stretches the muscles above the knee. To protect themselves from being stretched too far, the muscles respond by contracting, making the knee jerk.

The pupil of your eye shows another reflex reaction. If you shine a light into your eye, the pupil suddenly becomes much smaller, to prevent too much light entering. With a mirror and flashlight, you can see this reflex quite easily.

Testing reflex reactions

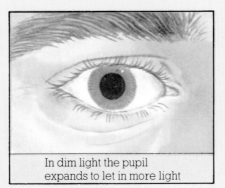

In dim light the pupil expands to let in more light

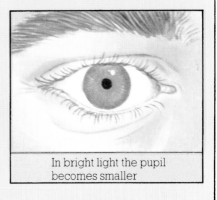

In bright light the pupil becomes smaller

Voluntary Control

The cells that make up the nervous system are called neurons. Each one has a cell-body and a main fiber. Neurons are connected to one another by tiny fibers called dentrites. There are two main classes of neurons. Those that send messages *from* the brain to make muscles work are called the motor neurons. Those that send information *to* the brain are the sensory neurons. When you thread a needle, your brain gets sensory information from your eyes and fingers, so that it can control your fine movements through motor nerves.

Threading a needle

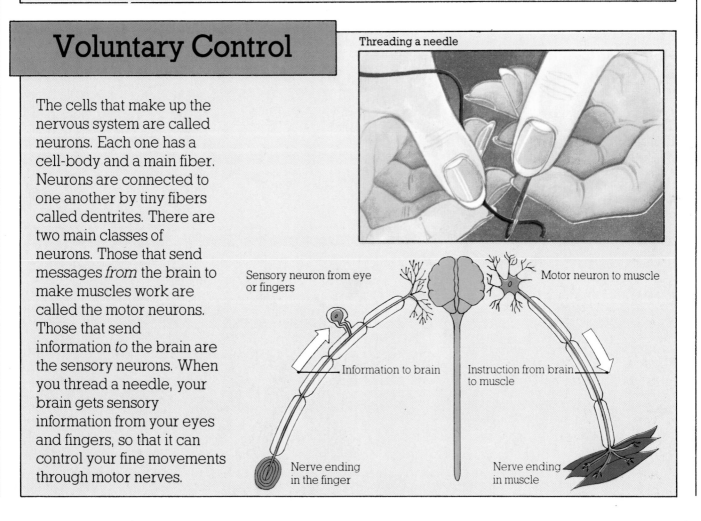

Sensory neuron from eye or fingers

Motor neuron to muscle

Information to brain

Instruction from brain to muscle

Nerve ending in the finger

Nerve ending in muscle

Sensing the Environment

Whether we are having an ordinary day, or whether we are out and about enjoying our favorite hobby, our experience of the outside world comes through our five senses: touch, taste, smell, hearing and sight.

Together, our senses give us a picture of our environment. Although we tend to concentrate on the information we get from our eyes and ears, we also pick up such things as the feel of the ground and the smells of the countryside. Even though we may not take much notice of these at the time, they are stored away in the brain, and probably help to make a day like the one this boy and girl are enjoying a lot more memorable than an ordinary one.

The activity of our senses is so important that very large parts of the brain are devoted to processing the information they get from the sense organs. The area at the back of each of the brain's hemispheres is concerned with processing information from the eyes, while an area almost as large at the side of each hemisphere is concerned with hearing. Because smell is less important to humans than to most other animals, only a small proportion of the brain is given over to it. The sensory nerves in the skin carry feelings such as pressure, heat, cold, dryness and dampness back to the brain. This information is dealt with in another specialized area in the middle of the cerebral hemispheres.

▷ Our senses pick up information about our environment. During a day's birdwatching, the senses of sight and hearing are most important, but the others – smell, taste and touch – also add to the experience.

The senses

Lying on the ground and looking at the birds, this boy is making most use of three of his senses. He is using his eyes to observe the geese, and his ears to hear their calls and those of other birds. He is also using his sense of touch, which makes him aware of such things as the feel of the grass and the amount of pressure he is putting on his elbows. The girl is using her senses of smell, taste, sight and hearing as she picnics.

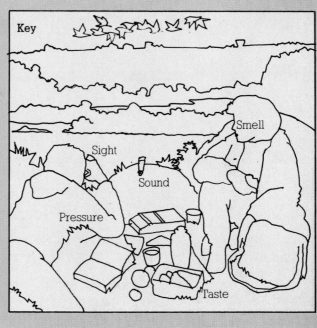

Key

Sight

Sound

Smell

Pressure

Taste

Seeing

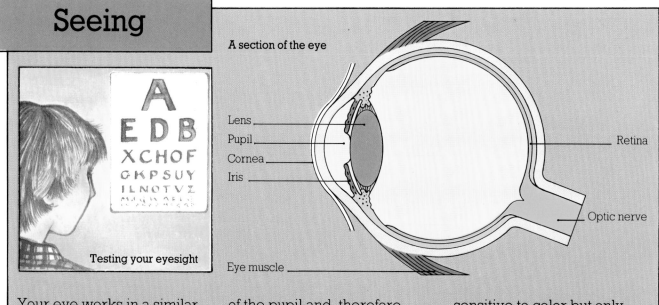

Testing your eyesight

A section of the eye

Lens
Pupil
Cornea
Iris
Retina
Optic nerve
Eye muscle

Your eye works in a similar way to a camera. Light passes through a transparent "window" – the cornea – and the fluid-filled space behind it to the lens. The iris is a muscle that lies in front of the lens and controls the size of the pupil and, therefore, the amount of light that passes through the lens. The lens changes shape to focus the light on the retina, which consists of a "carpet" of light- and color-sensitive cells. These cells are of two types: cones, which are sensitive to color but only function in good light; and rods, which are highly sensitive to even small amounts of light, but which are color blind. Signals from these cells travel down the thick optic nerve to the brain.

Hearing

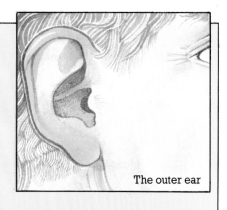

The outer ear

Sound consists of pressure waves in the air. The pitch and loudness of these waves make up the characteristics of an individual sound. The outer ear picks up these waves and they set up vibrations in the ear drum. These vibrations are carried across the space of the middle ear by three tiny ear bones.

These bones vibrate, sending the sound waves to the fluid-filled inner ear, or cochlea. The cochlea contains special cells that are sensitive to vibration. These cells pick up the pitch and power of the original sound.

The semicircular canals are also a part of the inner ear. They pick up any movement of the head, giving the brain information that helps keep the body balanced.

A diagrammatic section of the ear

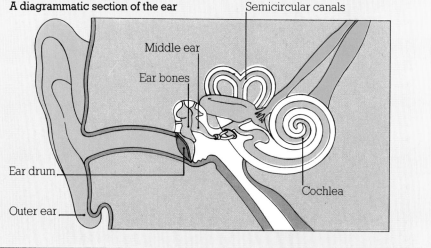

Semicircular canals
Middle ear
Ear bones
Ear drum
Outer ear
Cochlea

Feeling

Ouch!

A section of the skin

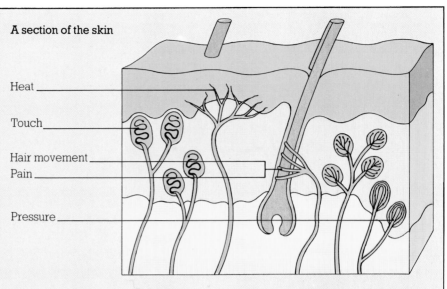

Heat

Touch

Hair movement

Pain

Pressure

Our skin is very sensitive to many different types of sensations. Not only can we tell the difference between hot and cold, but we can also differentiate between rough and smooth textures and feel even the lightest touch.

In fact, the skin has different sorts of "receptors," located at the end of the sensory nerves. A light touch will trigger a response from one type of receptor, while heavy pressure will set off another. Others register heat or pain.

Some parts of the skin are much more richly supplied with nerve endings than others, making them much more sensitive. The lips and inside of the mouth and the fingertips are especially sensitive areas.

Taste and Smell

The senses of taste and smell are very closely linked. In the upper part of the nose there are sensitive cells that react to thousands of different chemicals. The nerves from these cells communicate directly with the brain.

Most of the flavors that we appreciate when we are eating are the result of these "smell" nerves being stimulated. The tongue, with its special nerves of taste, is only able to appreciate the basic flavors of salty, bitter, sweet and sour. Each taste is picked up by a separate area of the tongue.

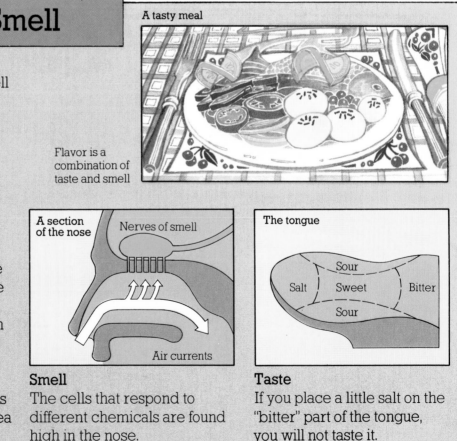

A tasty meal

Flavor is a combination of taste and smell

A section of the nose

Nerves of smell

Air currents

The tongue

Sour

Salt | Sweet | Bitter

Sour

Smell
The cells that respond to different chemicals are found high in the nose.

Taste
If you place a little salt on the "bitter" part of the tongue, you will not taste it.

Medical Aid

This boy had an attack of appendicitis. The appendix is a small "pouch" at the beginning of the large intestine. If it becomes inflamed, it can damage other areas. In extreme cases the appendix bursts, spreading infected material inside the abdomen.

When appendicitis occurs, an operation is necessary to remove the diseased appendix. After the operation the patient has to recover not only from the effects of the surgery, but also from the effects of abdominal infection. After an abdominal operation, the intestines are not able to work for a day or two, so the patient will not be able to eat for a while. However, the body still needs fluids, and these are given through a tube into the arm.

If patients are constantly worrying about themselves, they are unlikely to make a speedy recovery. Friends and members of the family play an important part in aiding recovery by visiting to give support and encouragement.

Although patients normally remain in bed immediately after the operation, the nurses will encourage them to get up and around at the earliest possible moment. This will assist them in their recovery and will also stop the muscles weakening and wasting, a situation that occurs when people have to stay in bed for a long time. In the days that follow the operation, doctors will monitor all of the body's systems, to check that recovery is taking place as expected.

▷ For the first two or three days after an operation, the patient needs as much rest as possible. Everyone keeps a close check on him to see that the wound is healing as it should and the body is making a good recovery from the effects of surgery.

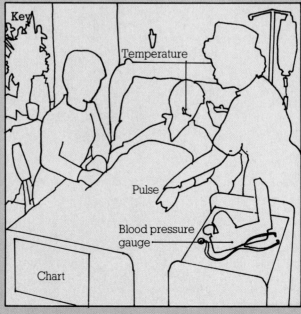

The body's recovery
By making different observations, the nurse can make sure that all the body's systems are working together to make the patient healthy. She takes his temperature to see if there is any infection remaining. When she takes his blood pressure and pulse, she is checking for any change in the action of the heart. This will also show whether the infection has gone. All these things are recorded on the patient's chart fixed at the foot of the bed.

Key

Temperature

Pulse

Blood pressure gauge

Chart

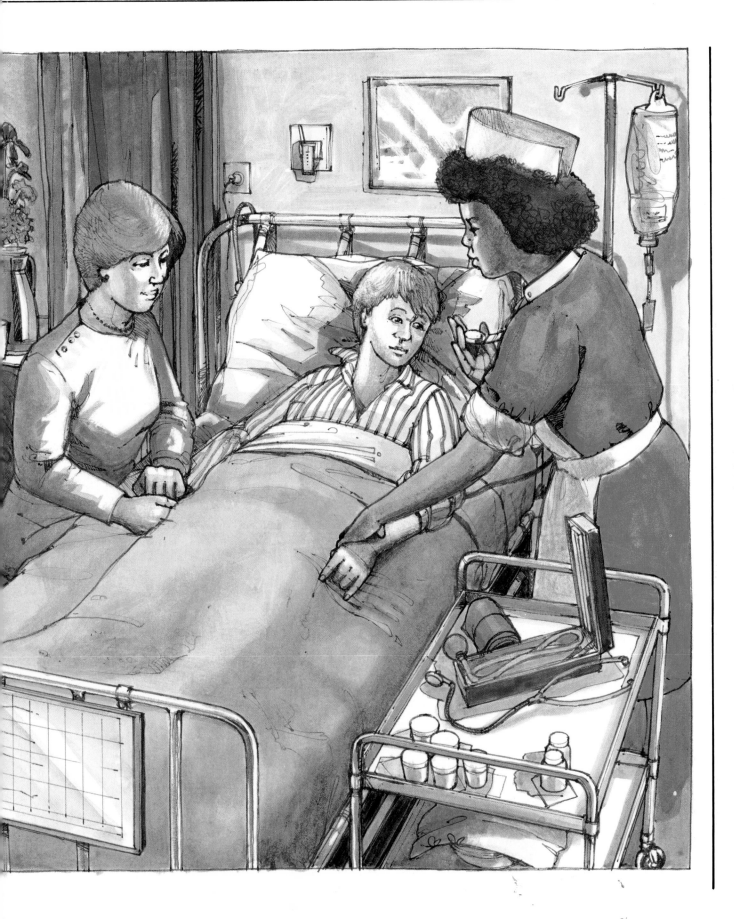

Invaders

A microscopic view of viruses

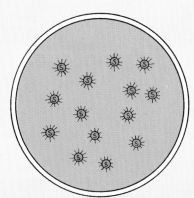

A microscopic view of bacteria

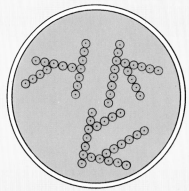

A microscopic view of protozoa

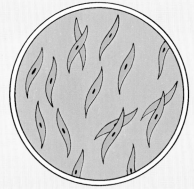

Viruses

Minor illnesses such as colds and flu, as well as more serious ones, are caused by viruses. They are so small that they can be seen only with the most powerful microscopes. They live inside the cells that they invade.

Bacteria

Bacteria are larger than viruses and can be seen with an ordinary microscope. They cause many different infections, including those that cause high temperatures, or diarrhea and vomiting.

Protozoa

Protozoa, such as the malaria parasite, are responsible for many infections, particularly in hot, tropical climates. Like malaria, many protozoa are passed from human to human by the bite of an infected insect.

Inner Defenses

Any invader first has to get past the body's outer defenses. The most important of these are the skin, the eye membranes, and mucous membranes in the mouth and nose.

Air passages are also protected by cilia (fine hair-like structures). These move back and forth, sweeping up dust and other invaders that are either sneezed or coughed away or swallowed.

Suffering from a cold

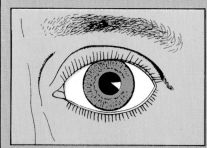

Skin and conjunctivae
The skin and conjunctivae (eye membranes) keep many invaders out.

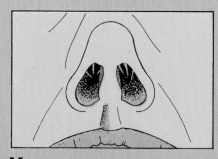

Mucus
Membranes of the air passages are protected by the mucus and cilia.

Stomach acid
Most invaders that are swallowed are destroyed by the stomach acid.

Outer Defenses

Although the body has effective outer defenses, organisms can still get in, especially at cuts and grazes. The job of protecting the body from invaders once they have got through the outer defenses is done by the immune defense system. This relies on the effects of different white blood cells to protect the body.

The lymphocytes, one of the two main classes of white blood cell, are the most important cells within the immune system. They make antibodies – special chemicals that "lock" on to an invader. They are also responsible for recognizing an invader in the tissues.

Destroying an invader

The first step in destroying an invader is that it should be recognized. This is shown in diagram (1). In diagram (2) the lymphocyte is starting to make antibodies, which have locked on to the invader in diagram (3). The antibodies themselves have a number of different functions. Simply by binding on to some invaders, they stop them from doing any damage. The final attack on an invading organism is made by a phagocyte (4). These cells engulf invaders that have been attacked by antibodies first. Once engulfed by a phagocyte, the organism is destroyed inside the phagocyte cell (5).

A nasty blow

1 Invader recognized

2 Antibodies released

3 Antibodies attach to invader

4 Phagocyte attacks invader

5 Invader destroyed

Immunity

Before our immune system can produce effective antibodies to an invading organism, the antibody-producing cells must have come into contact with the invader on a previous occasion. This is why people usually become "immune" to diseases such as measles and chicken pox after they have had an attack. But people can become immune to a particular organism without making the patient suffer from the ill effects of the disease. This is done by the technique of active immunization or vaccination.

Feeding baby

Small babies have very little resistance to infection. However, many of the antibodies from the mother's body are transferred in her milk. This gives the baby protection against infection, unlike bottle feeding.

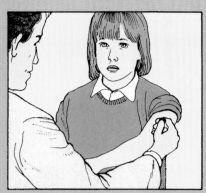
A vaccination

With active immunization, a vaccine stimulates the body to make antibodies. The vaccine either contains dead organisms, or live ones that have been treated so that they will not cause any symptoms.

Diagnosing Disease

It is better to try to prevent disease using techniques such as immunization, rather than to try to cure them as they occur. But unfortunately, many diseases cannot yet be prevented.

Most doctors spend their time attempting to cure diseases, or at least to relieve the symptoms they cause. In order to look after someone in this way, doctors must know exactly which disease they are dealing with – they must make a diagnosis. This is done by listening to the patient talk about the symptoms and by examining him or her for signs of disease.

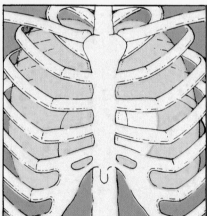
An X ray

More and more, special tests and investigations are used to confirm the diagnosis or to see if treatment is working. The X ray, a kind of photograph of internal structures, is just one of a great many tests that doctors make.

Using a stethoscope

Often, the first stage of a diagnosis is an examination by the family doctor. Here the doctor is using a stethoscope to listen to the chest. With this she can find out if there is anything wrong with the heart or lungs.

Surgery

Surgery is one of the most dramatic ways of curing an illness. However, even to take out an appendix, a surgeon needs a team of people to help him. There will probably be both a nurse and another doctor assisting with the actual surgery. Perhaps the most important support is provided by the anesthetist. A modern anesthetist does much more than just keep the patient asleep. For example, he makes sure the abdomen is relaxed so that the operative maneuvers can be performed. Infection must be prevented at all costs, so the instruments and the outer clothes of the surgeon and his associates are provided in sterile packs.

Inside an operating room

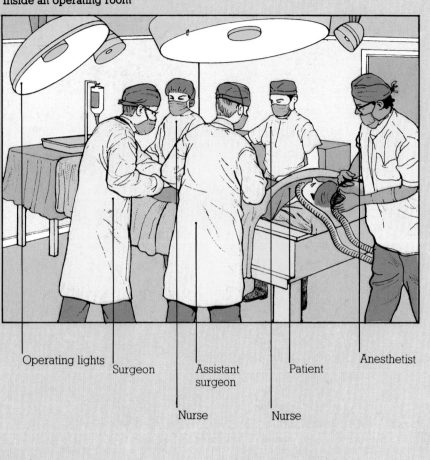

Operating lights   Surgeon   Assistant surgeon   Patient   Anesthetist

Nurse   Nurse

Recovery and Care

In the 1930s, a doctor only had about half a dozen drugs to use to combat disease. Today's doctor has thousands. Perhaps the most important of these are the antibiotics. These drugs kill infectious organisms without harming the patient. Many once fatal diseases can now be treated quickly and effectively with antibiotics. Other drugs relieve symptoms of disease, allowing patients to lead normal lives.

Recovering in bed

A Healthy Life

Probably the best way to prevent disease would be to check everyone at regular intervals for early signs of problems – a process called screening. Screening is especially effective soon after birth, when problems can be treated early, avoiding lasting damage. Keeping a check on the way young babies gain weight gives a good indication of their general health.

Screening and preventive treatment is particularly effective in dentistry. With regular checkups, the dentist picks up early signs of decay while most of the tooth is still healthy. The decay results from infection, and the decayed part can be removed and replaced by a filling. But preventive treatment also includes regularly brushing our teeth with fluoride toothpaste and not eating too much sugar.

Heart attacks and strokes cause a large number of deaths in Western countries. High blood pressure greatly increases the risk of both problems, and treatment of high blood pressure by reducing salt intake reduces this risk. A simple blood pressure measurement is the most effective screening test. However, smoking is just as important a risk as high blood pressure, and one much easier to avoid.

Watching early development

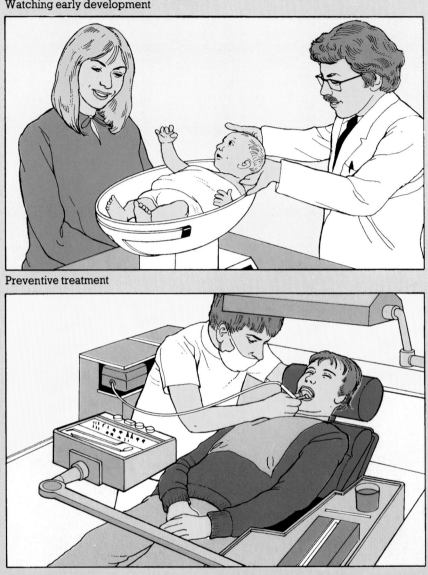

Preventive treatment

A regular checkup

Preventing Disease

Preventing and curing disease in an individual can do a great deal to increase the health of the community. But the greatest impact on community health has been made by educating people about simple diet and hygiene measures, and by providing things such as effective drains and a clean water supply. Both of these dramatically cut the amount of infection in the community. Much less progress has been made in preventing diseases not related to infection. Reducing alcohol drinking and cigarette smoking would greatly reduce many liver, heart and lung diseases.

Personal hygiene

Many bacteria are passed out of the body in feces. If food is contaminated with these bacteria, there is a high risk of infection. Washing your hands after using the bathroom is a very important aspect of personal hygiene.

Hygiene in the home

Bacteria grow best in warm conditions, so refrigerating food reduces the risk of infection. If food is covered, the risk of contamination by bacteria carried by flies is also reduced. Utensils used in food preparation must be scrupulously clean.

Destroying Disease

One of the most spectacular achievements of modern medicine has been the eradication of smallpox, once one of man's greatest enemies. There has not been a known case of the disease anywhere in the world since 1978. Apart from specimens kept in medical laboratories, the smallpox virus is now extinct. The eradication of smallpox is the result of worldwide cooperation through the World Health Organization. It depended on two things – isolation and immunization.

Isolation ward

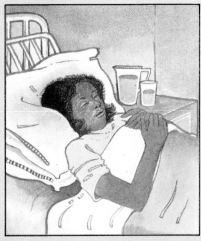

Isolation
The early recognition and isolation of smallpox cases was vital to prevent the spread of the disease

Mass immunization

With the development of a safe smallpox vaccine, whole populations were made immune to the disease.

Glossary

Abdomen   The central part of the body between the chest and the pelvis. The abdomen contains the organs of digestion, including the stomach and intestines, and other organs such as the kidneys and liver.

Antibody   A chemical produced by the body's immune (defense) system, which attaches itself to an invading organism and destroys it, so helping the body to defend itself against infection.

Arteries   The thick-walled blood vessels that carry blood from the heart to the rest of the body.

Capillaries   Tiny, thin-walled blood vessels which take blood from the arteries and deliver it to the cells.

Enzyme   A substance made by the cells that triggers off chemical reactions. Some enzymes mix with food in the small intestine to help digestion.

Ligaments   The tough fibrous bands that hold bones together.

Lymphocyte   One of the major types of white blood cell. The lymphocytes are especially important in recognizing invaders and in starting off the production of the antibodies which attack them.

Neurons   The cells that make up the nervous system.

Organism   Any living thing is an organism. The word is usually used in medicine to refer to the viruses, bacteria and other invaders that cause infection.

Pelvis   The bony girdle at the base of the abdomen and the point at which the legs are attached to the trunk of the body.

Phagocyte   A white blood cell that is capable of engulfing invading organisms.

Reflex   An action of the nervous system that does not depend upon our conscious control, but that happens automatically. Doctors use the reflexes to look for problems in the nervous system.

Scapula   The shoulder blade. A flat triangular bone.

Tendon   The fibrous material that binds muscles to bones.

Veins   Blood vessels that carry blood back to the heart from the rest of the body. Veins have thinner walls than arteries.

Vertebra   One of the bones which form the spine.

Index

PRINTED IN BELGIUM BY

proost

INTERNATIONAL BOOK PRODUCTION